CW00521563

Lincoln

in old picture postcards

by
David Cuppleditch

European Library - Zaltbommel/Netherlands MCMLXXXIV

Dedication:
For the Dean of Lincoln, Oliver Twistleton Wickham Fiennes, who taught me at Clifton College.

Acknowledgements:
Not being a postcard collector myself, I am much indebted to Harold Smith, Charles Smith, Richard Mawer, Brian Clarke, George Exley, Norman Cawkwell and Catherine Wilson of the 'Museum of Lincolnshire Life' for lending me certain cards used in this volume. A special thanks goes to Ken Atterby of Northgate Studios once again for his excellent photography. Last but not least I am very grateful to Fred Morton, a Lincoln journalist, for all his invaluable help.

GB   ISBN 90 288 2840 0

European Library in Zaltbommel/Netherlands publishes among other things the following series:

IN OLD PICTURE POSTCARDS *is a series of books which sets out to show what a particular place looked like and what life was like in Victorian and Edwardian times. A book about virtually every town in the United Kingdom is to be published in this series. By the end of this year about 175 different volumes will have appeared. 1,250 books have already been published devoted to the Netherlands with the title* **In oude ansichten.** *In Germany, Austria and Switzerland 500, 60 and 15 books have been published as* **In alten Ansichten;** *in France by the name* **En cartes postales anciennes** *and in Belgium as* **En cartes postales anciennes** *and/or* **In oude prentkaarten** *150 respectively 400 volumes have been published.*

For further particulars about published or forthcoming books, apply to your bookseller or direct to the publisher.

This edition has been printed and bound by Grafisch Bedrijf De Steigerpoort in Zaltbommel/Netherlands.

INTRODUCTION

In this slim volume I have tried to portray a picture of Lincoln as it was — a jewel in Edwardian sunlight — or the sort of city that bustled with trade and yet still found time to be polite. That is the Lincoln I remember and I am glad to say with few exceptions it is still the same today. Lincoln retains that rare commodity these days, friendliness which, with its sense of history gives it a great deal of charm. Of course it would be impossible to write a book about Lincoln and not include at least part of its lengthy and distinguished past; the city simply oozes history from every pore.

Which ever way you approach Lincoln, the view of the cathedral is breathtaking and no doubt inspired Peter De Wint to paint it so many times. Mr. Martineau, who did much fine work for the magazine 'Lincolnshire Life', once said 'Many books would be needed to describe the wonders of this cathedral' and I can only agree with his sentiment, for Lincoln cathedral has to be seen to be appreciated. Whether glittering in sunshine or shrouded in mist, the majestic towers loom up from the summit of the hill, making it a sight which people seldom forget.

There have been numerous characters to add colour and variety to the city. For example John Banks Smith was known locally as 'Cuckoo' Smith because he sold a comic paper called the Cuckoo. Touting his periodical through the streets crying 'Cuckoo!' inevitably he attracted crowds of small boys and urchins all imitating him. Although his jacket and trousers were in a poor state of repair, he still wore a silk topper and it was said that he had been 'well off' at one time owning his own carriage and pair. There was also 'Torksey

Ned', a disreputable looking character who wore a battered top hat, tied with string underneath his chin. But it was more than a hat for underneath it was kept his next meal. He could usually be found on the steps of the old Butter Market devouring his lunch from its strange receptacle.

A popular pair was 'Fiddler Joe' and his wife who would tour the public houses in the city centre (and there were dozens of them). She sang while he scratched at an old violin. Their repertoire which consisted of two ditties only, 'Down among the coal' and 'Pop! Goes the Weasel' seemed a bit limited but the public liked them. Another favourite character was Frank Walker, who had a bakery and shop on Waterside North near High Bridge. Better known as 'Pie' Walker, his speciality was selling hot pies and gravy which he would hawk about the streets keeping them warm with a coke fire on a barrow. His delicious pies were 'tuppence' each!

An old tramp with no special claim to fame was 'Louth Joe', who attracted crowds of annoying children. He abused his tormentors so much that at a local County Council Meeting someone suggested that he should be locked up. 'He should be put away if he's not fit to be about,' said a councillor, 'And if he's fit to be about he should be protected.' In the event the police were given instructions to keep an eye on him and to see that he was not molested.

Apart from these eccentrics there was a more notable side to Lincolns distinguished past. It would appear that on the other side of the coin most of the memorable people were connected with the cathedral. Running through the Bishops of Lincoln we find St. Hugh, Grosseteste, John of Dalderby,

Dr. Oliver Sutton, Richard Flemmyng, Richard Reynolds, Dr. Christopher Wordsworth and Dr. Edward King. They all added their own contributions to maintaining and enhancing the glory of Lincoln cathedral.

Of the others who were not directly connected with the cathedral there was Dr. Richard Smith, who founded Christ's Hospital, Lincoln, and Sir William Monson (1559-1643), who was knighted at the Seige of Cadiz, and Brevet-Major Bromhead, who resided at Thurlby near Lincoln and was the hero of Rorke's Drift, Zululand, on January 22nd 1879. More recently those popular T.V. and radio personalities Steve Race and Keith Fordyce (whose real name is Marriott) and the Middle East correspondant for the BBC, Keith Graves, were all born and brought up in Lincoln.

One of the most dynamic M.P.'s that Lincoln has ever had was Dick Taverne, an able and thoroughly honest politician (a rarity). I first met him in the mid-seventies and one evening he explained the concept of a totally new party in British politics — quite frankly I didn't believe him. However, some years later the party he was talking about came into being, this was the SDP. Taverne hit the headlines in the early seventies when he saw flaws in the Labour Party, stood as an Independant for Lincoln, and won.

In complete contrast an earlier Lincoln M.P. was the forth-right Colonel Charles Sibthorp, an arch Tory. Full of self importance, he served as a constant target for the cartoonists of the day. Sibthorp inherited Canwick Hall and was responsible for the hand rail being placed halfway up steep hill. This prevented anyone from trying to emulate the feat which he undertook of driving a 'four in hand' down the severe gradient of Steep Hill for a wager.

All these characters have given Lincoln a living history. Their contributions peppered with certain idiosyncrasies have helped to mould this very individual society. Like the amiable hostelries that are generously pinpointed around the city, Lincoln has extended an unremitting hospitality to all who have gone there. Luckily this has been preserved in excellent photographic records and postcards which now gives us the chance to reflect on Lincoln's immediate past with both its glories and its shortcomings.

There seems to be something of a boom in nostalgia just at the moment, with various publications either specialising in or vaguely connected with events that occurred years ago. This interest has sparked off a glut of amateur historians scurrying to their desks and reeling off page after page of interminable tripe. Fortunately Lincoln has emerged unscathed from this onslaught and instead has only been blessed with publications of the highest standard. Sir Francis Hill's authoritative volumes on the city (four in all) cover periods of Lincoln's history in a scholarly fashion. Not to be forgotten is Abell and Chambers potted history, entitled 'The Story of Lincoln' and published in 1939 by the City of Lincoln Education Committee. More recently Messrs. Elvin and Hodgson have added their own individual touches to an increasing collection and I hope that this small book will be yet another useful addition to the volumes already compiled.

1. This view of Lincoln cathedral from the south-west has undoubtedly been the most popular choice of photographers for the last hundred years. It has been reproduced on numerous calendars, postcards, mugs and ashtrays and portrays the three towers to good advantage.

2. Lincoln cathedral was founded by Remigius (the first Bishop of Lincoln), who came over to England with William the Conqueror in 1066. However, the cathedral only had a short existence being shattered by the great earthquake of 1185 which split it in two from top to bottom.

3. Bishop Hugh commenced rebuilding the present structure using some remains of Remigius' original Norman building in the western façade.

4. The Norman doorways of Bishop Remigius' original west front were richly ornamented by Bishop Alexander in the twelfth century as can be seen in the postcard. The arches have since been repaired and cleaned and unfortunately the old fashioned gas lamps, which stood on the pavement outside, have been removed.

5. This picturesque view of the cathedral, showing the grand central tower from James Street, has changed remarkably little since this postcard was produced in the twenties. Depicting a charming peep down an ivy clad and cobbled street, it was one of the few postcards produced by that well-known postcard company Judges of Hastings. Incidentally the central tower houses the 'Great Tom' bell originally cast in 1610 (and recast in 1834) which weighs considerably over five tons!

ST. HÜGH.

From the S. W. Pinnacle of Lincoln Cathedral.

Probably the best likeness in existence

Erected A.D. 1200.

6. The historian Froude called Bishop Hugh 'one of the true builders of our nations greatness' whilst the common people said of him that he was 'the hammer of kings'. And it would appear that when Bishop Hugh of Avalon died in 1200 he was held in high esteem. At his funeral King John of England and King William of Scotland were among the pall bearers and over one hundred abbots were present amongst a host of Earls, Bishops and Barons.

7. Lincolnshire has never made much of the fact that Alfred Lord Tennyson was born in the county and that he spent his formative years roaming in and around the Lincolnshire countryside. A few plaques littered sparingly about, a statue in the grounds of Lincoln cathedral and a separate room in the Usher Art Gallery are the only artefacts to remind us that this giant of English literature had any connections with the county at all. Fortunately there is a flourishing Tennyson Society trying to rectify this; students from all over the world visit the Tennyson Centre at the Central Library. This particular statue at the north-east of the cathedral was sculpted by his friend G.F. Watts (who was better known as a Victorian painter) and shows Tennyson admiring a wayside flower.

The Tennyson Memorial, LINCOLN.

Flower in the crannied wall,
I pluck you out of the crannies:
I hold you here, root and all, in my hand
Little flower—but if I could understand
What you are, root and all, and all in all
I should know what God and man is.

GRECIAN STAIRS LINCOLN

8. Leading down from the cathedral to Lindum Road is an attractive stairway commonly known as the Grecian Stairs. In fact the correct name for this sort cut should be the 'Greesen Stairs' (which came from Grees meaning steps in mediaeval English). Also there is an old graveyard at the top of the stairs from the church of St. Margaret-in-the-Close which was demolished in 1774.

9. This view of Castle Hill and Exchequergate, with the misty towers of the west front looming in the background, has long been a popular view with artists. Turner did a particularly fine painting of it. There used to be little shops selling beads, rosaries and similar ecclesiastical hardware in pre-Reformation days in the arches of the Exchequer and also a pub known as 'The Great Tom Inn'. The rooms above these shops were originally offices dealing with Exchequer business connected with the cathedral — hence the name Exchequergate.

10. On 9th June 1910, Lincoln was honoured by a visit from Sir Edward Elgar when he came to conduct 'The Dream of Gerontius' in the cathedral. He is pictured here standing, second from the right, along with some of the musical soloists. The gentleman standing on the far left is Mr. Gervase Elwes from the talented Elwes family of Elsham Hall. This picture was taken in Dr. Bennett's garden in Northgate. Dr. Bennett was the cathedral organist and master of the choristers, seen here sitting in the deck chair.

11. Edward King, Bishop of Lincoln (1885-1910), was a well respected man, loved by all who met him and deeply missed when he died. King was responsible for moving the Bishops Palace from Riseholme (now an agricultural college) back to Lincoln. His predecessor Bishop Wordsworth (1869-1885) had spent his entire episcopate at Riseholme. (Wordsworth was nephew of the poet, William Wordsworth.) The proceeds of the sale of Riseholme helped to pay for the new Bishops Palace which was designed by Ewan Christian. Now known as Edward King House, it is a pleasant ecumenical conference centre serving bed and breakfast. Meanwhile the Bishop's Residence has moved again; in 1945 it moved to Eastgate where it remains today.

12. Bishop Alnwick's tower was part of the ancient palace and just to the right of Edward King House. It is more or less the same today although the ivy growths have been removed and the surrounding grounds are tendered. In 1954 these ruins were taken into the care of the Ministry of Public Buildings and Works (later known as the Department of the Environment) and are now open to the public on certain days.

13. Portraits of Edward King including etchings, oils, prints and photographs are ubiquitous around Lincoln. On the reverse side of this postcard it says 'How do you like our old friend here? — It is a *good* one of him.' One touching story regarding money demonstrates why so many people loved him. Because he was a bachelor, Edward King's mother kept house which included looking after the servants. She was constantly amazed that her servants did not complain about their wages when so many others did, but Edward King had an arrangement with them. He is reputed to have said 'Take the little brown envelope my mother gives you (ie their wages) and then come and see me later.'

THE CASTLE, LINCOLN.

6a

14. Much of Castle Gateway is structurally Norman, but is hidden by the alterations which were made in the fourteenth century. Between the inner and outer gates is a fine oriel window brought from John O'Gaunts Palace (now demolished) for preservation. Here also is a fragment of the first of the Eleanor Crosses which stood near Cross O'Cliff Hill at the southern end of the city. On the right of the gateway in this postcard is the observatory tower which boasts possibly the finest panorama of the city available to the public.

15. Lincoln castle was built in 1068 by William the Conqueror to keep a hold on the English. Nearly two hundred homes were cleared to make way for it, many of which had Roman foundations. Out of the houses that surround the castle today sadly Ellis' Brewery, Drury Lane, has gone but the majority remain.

16. The only entrance into the castle is here (through the eastern gate). This photograph was taken before it was cleaned up some years ago; the ivy and other arborial growths which were eating into the ancient stonework posed a real threat. Once inside the castle the County Hall and Assize Courts are directly opposite; they were built in 1826 at a cost of £40,000. To the left of this postcard is Castle Hill House.

17. Behind Castle Hill House (a comfortable family home) could be found this splendid garden. It was the residence of Dr. J. Stitt-Thomson and portions of the house dated back to the fourteenth century. Unfortunately it was demolished some years ago and the site is now a municipal car park.

CASTLE GATEWAY, LINCOLN.

Copyright

18. Another view of the castle gateway showing a particularly fine half timbered building (just to the right of this picture) which was restored by the National Provincial Bank in 1929 and which is now a Tourist Information Centre.

19. Just in front of the castle was the Black Boy Inn (now the Castle Club). At a time when carrier carts and country waggons came into Lincoln to sell their wares in Castle Square, the Black Boy Inn enjoyed a flourishing trade. Marwood the executioner used to stay here when he had duties to perform in the castle and a bellringers jack used to be housed in this pub. It was presented to the inn by Alderman Bullen in 1782 for safekeeping, but when the pub closed it was moved to Brighton. Incidentally this hostelry was a favourite haunt of bellringers who used to partake of a noggin after their sessions.

20. In Victorian times it was customary to hold the annual Mayoral Garden Party in the castle grounds, as this postcard shows. The red brick prison to the right of the picture was built in 1787 and enlarged in 1845. It was the prison, governor's residence until 1878. Behind this is the prison chapel, a curious and fascinating reminder of bygone days.

The Prison Chapel
Lincoln Castle.

21. Surely a most unusual subject — for a holiday postcard. The pews of the prison chapel were specially designed to allow the prisoners to see the chaplain in his pulpit without seeing each other. Each prisoner stood or sat in these wooden compartments and had to be locked in before the next prisoner was admitted. Condemned criminals sat at the back, women at the front and debtors at the side.

22. This idyllic rural picture of a thrashing machine at work, near Lincoln, symbolises the real importance of Lincoln's wealth in the nineteenth century. Clayton and Shuttleworth were the first firm to place a portable engine in the hands of farmers which was not too complex for everyday use and which saved much arduous work. Up to this time threshing had been done by hand, but in 1850 Lincoln suddenly became an industrial goldmine. With these new labour saving devices and other steam worked implements selling as quickly as they came off the production line, other firms soon sprang up, such as Ruston, Proctor and Co., Robey and Co. and W. Foster and Co.

23. During the First World War, Lincoln firms were quick to aid the war effort. The first tanks were made at Lincoln under the surprising name of 'Water carriers for Mesopotamia' to disguise their real intention. Aircraft too were churned out by the dozen; Ruston, Proctor and Co. kept the Royal Air Force supplied with Sopwith Camels whilst Clayton and Shuttleworth made Tri-planes. The aircraft in this postcard was a Robey Short 184 sea plane and it was exhibited in the Great Northern Goods Yard in 1916.

24. Workers scurrying home after a hard days toil at Ruston, Proctor and Co. on Waterside South. Joseph Ruston joined the company in 1857 and by 1918, largely due to his entrepreneureal talents, it had become the world well-known firm of Ruston and Hornsby (parts of which are still operative today).

25. Delivering milk and parcels from the central railway (circa 1905). In the days before our daily pinta it was quite usual for the milkman to deliver milk in churns and pour it out into a container on your doorstep. However, what I like about this postcard is the cheeky grin on the young lads face.

26. On 2nd December 1904 a case of typhoid was officially confirmed in Lincoln. By the end of January 1905 nearly 350 cases had been notified and as the epidemic increased over a thousand cases were confirmed with approximately 130 fatalities. This horrible infection gripped the city and temporary hospitals soon sprang up in churches, chapels and the Drill Hall in Broadgate. The cause of this raging epidemic was of course the water supply. Eventually Lincoln Corporation managed to arrange an alternative source of water via Elkesley in Nottinghamshire. This postcard shows a group mostly comprised of youngsters carrying their buckets to collect some pure water which was kindly delivered from neighbouring Newark. The poster in the background is advertising Bainbridges Store in High Street. Incidentally Lincoln still takes its water from Elkesley, the supply being first connected in 1911.

THE KING ARRIVING AT THE ROYAL SHOW, LINCOLN. JUNE 26th 1907.

27. It was a red letter day for Lincoln when King Edward VII paid an official visit to the Royal Show on 25th June 1907, accompanied by the Grand Duke of Hesse and Prince Alfred of Greece. The Mayor, Mr. J. Ruston, dressed in all his regalia, went with the Royal party to the showground on West Common.

ROYAL PROCESSION, LINCOLN, 1907.   PHOTO - C. ASKEW.

28. Lincoln put on a blazing exhibition and brought out all its finery for the show. Also the event was well covered by the photographers of the day as this set of postcards clearly demonstrates.

29. Hundreds of people lined the streets just to catch a glimpse of this controversial Royal in his Landau. Faintly discernable in the background is the church of St. Mary-le-Wigford with the Queens Hotel on the right.

30. As the Royal personage passed down High Street underneath elaborately decorated arches sporting signs such as 'Lincoln's Wealth' and 'Lincoln's Fame' which were decked with the inevitable threshing machine on top of them, it must have occurred to many people that they had not seen a Royal let alone a King for a very long time indeed.

31. One of the reasons that Lincoln had been ignored by the Royal Family for so long was that Colonel Charles Sibthorp, who was an M.P. for Lincoln for most of his life, had taken umbrage to Prince Albert's annual allowance. When Albert was about to marry Victoria, Lord Melbourne, the then Prime Minister, had proposed to make Albert an annual allowance of £50,000. Colonel Sibthorp objected to this and the Prince Consort's allowance was eventually cut to £30,000. Queen Victoria was not amused.

Royal Agricultural Show, Lincoln. 1907.

P. JONES. LINCOLN.

32. This building was erected on West Common near to the racecourse just for the Show. (A part of the racecourse is visible in front of it.) Another feature of the Show was an ornamental pond which was laid out by Pennells, the local nursery, which can still be seen today.

33. When the Royal Show was over mopping up operations began. This was the view down High Street with banners still thronging the street and flags floating flaccidly overhead. It was possibly the largest and certainly the most significant that Lincoln has ever had.

34. High Street in the 1880's with the Spread Eagle Hotel on the right of the picture (with the elaborate Victorian lamp). The Trafford family managed this hotel from 1841 to 1898 when Thomas Lakin took over. In 1923 F.W. Woolworth bought the premises and converted it into one of their 'sixpenny stores'. The upper stories of the old frontage remained the same for many years until they were altered during World War II to mock Elizabethan. The most important aspect of this photograph concerns the carts and carriages which even then flocked to this part of Lincoln; these days it is a pedestrian precinct.

Stone Bow, Lincoln.

35. By the turn of the century much of the horse-drawn traffic had disappeared from High Street with bicycles, hand-drawn carts and pedestrians replacing them. The Saracen's Head Hotel, on the extreme right of the postcard, was one of the oldest hostelries in Lincoln. During the early part of the nineteenth century it had been a Post House for coaches to Peterborough and London; and during the Second World War the hotel was a favourite haunt of bomber crewmen, who frequently enjoyed a tipple or two in the Saracen's Head Bars. The Hotel closed in 1960 when all its contents were auctioned and is now Waring and Gillow, House Furnishers. Fortunately the ornate balcony still remains.

41042. LINCOLN: STONE BOW.

36. From Roman times there has always been a gate at the Stonebow. It was renewed in the four-teenth century and again in the sixteenth century when the present gatehouse was erected. The Guildhall above the arch has a fine timbered roof and contains some interesting portraits and City regalia. The City Prison used to adjoin this building until 1809 when it was moved.

37. In 1887 the Stonebow was repaired once again and double posterns were installed to replace the single ones. The double faced clock (on the top of the Stonebow) was presented in 1889 by F.H. Kerans M.P. whilst to the right of this (on the Guildhall roof) is the Mote bell, which dates from mediaeval times and is still rung to summon members of the council to meetings.

STONEBOW
& SALTERGATE,
LINCOLN.
—

SALTERGATE
LINCOLN.
13 MAY 1904.

fallen during alterations

J. W. RUDDOCK, PUBLISHER, LINCOLN.

38. Before Saltergate passage was widened in 1904, it was no bigger than an alleyway. This made Pratt and Sons (wine merchants) the corner building and, as you can see from this postcard, it was no mean task to demolish the pile.

39. Lincoln Horse Fair must have been a spectacular sight with horses standing on both sides of the High Street and only trotting down the middle of the road when would be purchasers wanted to see their paces. The annual fair, which also included a sheep and cattle market held behind the Grand Stand on the racecourse, took place during the last week in April. It was described in Whittaker's Almanack as the 'Greatest Fair in England'. Gypsy hostlers had a favourite trick of putting ginger around the rear end of the horses. This would automatically make the horses lively and therefore more alert and spirited in appearance, consequently fetching a higher price.

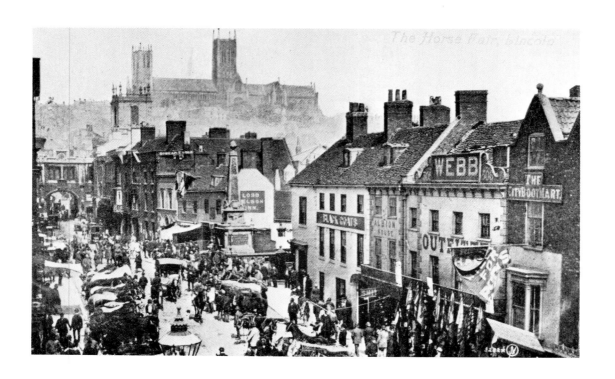

40. Because of increasing traffic problems the horse fair was transferred to West Common in 1929. During the Second World War it was moved once again to the cattle market and afterwards returned to West Common. But by 1952 not a single horse appeared for auction, and an ancient tradition ended.

41. During the week of Lincoln's Horse Fair there was also a pleasure fair on Monks Road for the more frivolous. This sparked off numerous private parties which gave youngsters an opportunity to dress up. Shown here is one such merry band taken near Lincoln. From the ingenious array of costumes it would appear that these youngsters were influenced by Gilbert and Sullivan's Mikado and coster girls of the day.

42. On High Bridge is the obelisk which was built to mark the site of the old chapel dedicated to St. Thomas of Canterbury. Work began on removing the obelisk because its weight was felt to be a danger to the Bridge, on the 15th February 1939. How the bridge withstood a chapel but not an obelisk is a puzzle!

43. Men at work in the latter part of the last century repairing the banks of Waterside North. The most noteable feature is that High Bridge had to be propped up with weighty timbers during this repair work to cope with the burden of the obelisk. Unfortunately this photograph is rather faded, but it demonstrates the urgency with which Victorian workmen went about their business.

44. This half-timbered building (off High Street), known as Whitefriars House, is a hundred yards or so south of the central level crossing. It was the subject of a heated debate in the city a few years ago when the old property on the south side of this narrow passage was being demolished to make way for a supermarket. There were strong objections to 'Burying' such a fine piece of architecture down a narrow dark passage, but the objections were overruled. The consequence is that comparatively few visitors see this attractive house these days.

LAST JOURNEY, LINCOLN HORSE TRAMS.
JULY 22ND 1905.

TO MEMORY DEAR.
REGISTERED.

45. The conversion from horse-drawn trams to the new electric powered trams seemed to be fairly painless, but even so it still took Lincoln Corporation five months to complete it. As the date on this postcard shows, trams must have been out of action from July 22nd to November 23rd in 1905. I wonder how long it would have taken to complete a similar conversion these days? Or indeed at what cost?

THE OPENING OF THE LINCOLN ELECTRIC TRAMWAYS. 23-11-05.

46. Amidst flags, shields and banners the new electric tram was given a cautious welcome. There was much resentment to this new form of transport as opposed to the affectionate old horse-drawn trams and it is not surprising because the new trams followed exactly the same route. As a poster of the time was to point out 'In affectionate remembrance of the Lincoln horse cars which succumbed to an electric shock after years of faithful service'; it added despondently that they were 'Gone But Not Forgotten'.

47. 'Welcome to the birthplace of the tanks' says the sign on this banner; and of course Lincoln played a very important role in both World Wars inventing, producing and modifying tanks in their hundreds. This particular photograph was taken circa 1919 of Fosters machine shop after the frantic activity of the war years.

48. William Fosters Hornet Tank on test for the government on a site just off Tritton Road. (Mr. W.A. Tritton, managing director of William Foster and Co., was later knighted and the road was named after him.) Under his able leadership Fosters designed and produced the worlds first tank, using the caterpillar track invented by Grantham industrialist David Roberts of Hornsby's. Apart from producing the Hornet, Fosters also made the Whippet and the appearance of these tanks boosted morale greatly on the front.

49. Fosters factory girls and staff seated in front of one of their Mark 1 tanks. The photograph illustrates a large female representation due to war time. This postcard was taken circa 1916 when the fighting was at its most fierce.

50. The Lincolnshire Yeomanry parading in what is now the courtyard of the Museum of Lincolnshire Life. Surprisingly this building (built 1856) is more or less the same today although the soft surface has been replaced by tarmac.

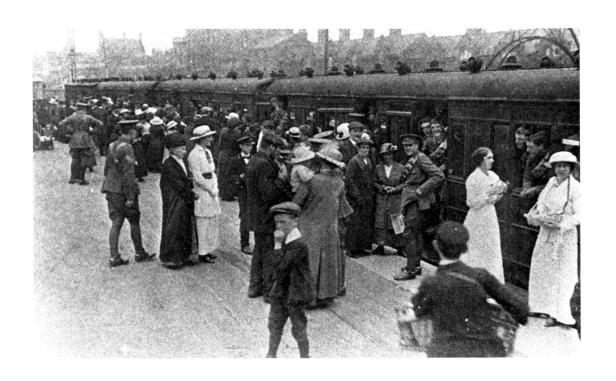

51. Soldiers of the Lincolnshire Yeomanry Regiment boarding a train at Lincoln Central Station (circa 1914) on the first leg of their journey abroad.

52. The last time the Sphinx cap badge was worn was on Monday 2nd March 1959, at a short ceremonial parade at the Depot Lincoln. The new East Anglian Brigade Badge replaced the Sphinx which commemorated the part played by the 10th Foot in the Nile Campaign of 1801. This is a postcard of a young raw recruit proudly sporting his Sphinx cap badge just before the First World War. I wonder if he ever came back?

53. On the 9th April 1918 King George V and Queen Mary visited Lincoln and their tour included a stop at the celebrated firm of Clayton and Shuttleworth's. They are pictured here with Mr. Alfred Shuttleworth (third from the right) with a Clayton 405 steam traction engine in the background.

GUARD OF HONOUR
TO THE KING,
LINCOLN,
APRIL 9TH 1918.

54. The Guard of Honour were made up mostly of invalid or infirm soldiers from the First World War. The one exception is the young seventeen year old Lance Corporal (second from right back row), who was Bob Powlesland. Originally he had trained as a pharmacist at Streets the Chemist's in Louth before joining up. Eventually he became a Major in the RAMC and went with the Expeditionary force to France in the Second World War where he was wounded and sent home. His next post was in Iceland where unfortunately he was killed on the 17th January 1942. On a particularly stormy night he went out walking with some of his fellow officers when a piece of corrugated iron roofing fell on him and he was decapitated; he was buried in the Fossvogur Cemetery, Reykjavik. The amazing thing about this postcard is that the Union Jack is upside down.

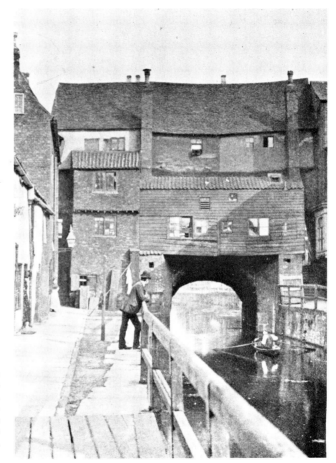

55. In this view of High Bridge before the alterations were made in 1901 there was a splendid back view looking up the Glory Hole. The bridge itself is about seven hundred years old and supposedly is the only mediaeval bridge left in England with houses still on it. Stokes Tea and Coffee Shop (one of the buildings on the bridge) used to waft the most glorious smells of freshly ground coffee down High Street to entice customers to sample their wares.

The "Glory Hole"
LINCOLN.

56. 'Jotter', the prolific postcard artist, visited Lincoln at the turn of the century and painted at least three views, including the Jews House, Exchequergate and this one of 'The Glory Hole'. 'Jotter', whose real name was Walter Hayward Young (1868-1920), often toured the British Isles in the company of his daughter Gwen, making delightful sketches of popular subjects which he treated in a chocolate box manner; this set of cards was produced for Boots the Chemist's in about 1906.

57. In the opposite direction to the Glory Hole was this view looking down the river Witham with Mayfield Bridge in the distance. Clearly depicting the shops and pubs which used to hug this once busy waterway it made a cosy picture. Barges brought in imports of timber and coal down this waterway and exported flour and grain from the cake mills of Doughty, Son and Richardson, and Henry Leetham. Now of course these buildings have been demolished only to be replaced with the ugly, impersonal back views of F.W. Woolworth on the leet and Burtons the Tailors and C&A on the right.

Brayford. *Lincoln.*

58. Brayford Pool was originally known as The Swanpool and the River Witham was not navigable under High Bridge until 1792. It was Sir Joseph Banks of Revesby who threatened to build a rival canal from Brayford to the Horncastle navigation canal that finally prompted Lincoln Corporation to do something about it.

59. The Brayford, as it is commonly known today, was one of the busiest parts of Lincoln in the last century. Formed by the confluence of the Fossdyke with the Upper Witham, it now serves as a mooring perch for luxury cruisers, tatty old boats and the corporation swans. Before the advent of the railway this was the heart of Lincoln. A host of wharves, warehouses, mills and coalyards sprang up around it, serving all the noteable firms with provisions and materials brought up from the Humber and Trent. There was even a steam packet which ran daily from Lincoln to Boston and back again, though it stopped short of Brayford Pool because of the impediment of High Bridge.

60. Broadgate leading up to Lindum Road with the cathedral in the background is very familiar to Lincolnians and visitors alike. Showing the drill hall on the left, which was built in 1890 on the site of Henry Newsum's timber works, and also the old Duke of Wellington public house, fourth from the left. The Duke of Wellington was demolished in 1932 to make way for a new edifice at the cost of several thousand pounds, nevertheless you can just detect the portrait of the Iron Duke on the sign outside this welcoming tavern.

61. To the right of Broadgate, at the junction with St. Rumbold Street, was the Wheatsheaf Inn. Surprisingly it still remains when so many buildings around it have been knocked down. John Bland was the first landlord in 1791 and from this photograph we see that it sold Halls Ely Ales and Stout opposed to the more usual Holes Newark Ales. But what I find so fascinating is the poster on the side of the wall. Mr. Ashton, the then proprietor, used to organise char-a-banc parties in the days before organised bus trips.

62. Looking down St. Rumbold Street, with the Wheatsheaf at the end on the right-hand side, we see an old chapel which is now the City and County Museum. In the middle distance is David Meggitt's (tin plate worker) whilst the old buildings on the right in the foreground have all been demolished to make way for a multi-storey car park. F. Applewhite's (motor body builders) is just visible.

63. Formerly this road was called New Road, but is now known as Lindum Road. Most of the houses at this time were occupied by leading traders and professional men. The building on the left is now Page & Co., solicitors, whilst the building next door to it is the headquarters of the Lincolnshire Red Cross Society; the third house has been demolished altogether. During the 1930's problems arose with the increased traffic both down Lindum Road and in Broadgate. Eventually the road was widened in the 1950's and a central reservation was placed in the thoroughfare. Even these measures have proved inadequate for modern traffic and soon a seven mile 'Lincoln Relief Road' will be built; much to everyones relief!

64. The Usher Art Gallery is unquestionably the most important gallery in the county. Lincoln Corporation bought No. 7 Lindum Road and Temple Gardens, a typical Victorian mansion belonging to the Collingham family (of Mawer and Collingham fame) as the site of their proposed new gallery. Temple Gardens, seen here, was a palatial family home with well laid out lawns and flower beds. The money for the new gallery came from a bequest by James Usher, who had amassed a fortune in his lifetime selling jewelry, watches and replicas of the Lincoln Imp. The Usher Art Gallery was officially opened on May 25th 1927 by Edward VIII (then Prince of Wales) in the presence of the Mayor and the Architect, Sir Reginald Blomfield.

LINCOLN. THE HIGH SCHOOL.

65. Half way up Lindum Road, known colloqually as Lindum Hill, was The Girls High School. Built in 1893 by Lincoln Architect William Watkins, who also designed the Constitutional Club in Silver Street, it is comprised of red brick and terra cotta. This unusual Victorian structure is now Lincoln College of Art.

66. Pottergate Arch has become a traffic island with roads running either side of it since this photograph was taken. The improvements, made in 1937, have no doubt helped to preserve this fine old antiquarian arch. It was called Pottergate because that a Roman supposedly once stood on this site. Incidentally the city arms have been incorporated into this postcard and although it was a common trait to blazon arms on many postcards, I have come across few bearing those of Lincoln.

67. This photograph of the Adam and Eve public house, just opposite Pottergate, was taken in 1922. At that time there were sheep grazing in the fields at the back of the pub in what is now the car park. During the early 1800's James Waites was the landlord and when he died in 1813 the contents of the pub were sold at auction; it was then discovered that he had 250 gallons of British gin in stock! Curiously two large marquees were also offered for sale and 'one small one', described as 'good as new, originally made for the Prince Regent's Gala and only used once', which indicates that he might also have done a bit of outside catering.

SITTING ROOM

ADAM AND EVE INN   LINCOLN

68. In 1841 the landlord of the Adam and Eve was Joseph Bateman (a name long associated with the brewery business in Lincolnshire). By 1885 the landlord was a Thomas Harrison, who by all accounts was something of a character. He was particularly fond of curios and objet d'art and made the pub into a sort of museum. Hanging old guns, swordfish blades, stuffed birds, bulls horns and pith helmets around the pub; it took on the appearance of a cluttered Victorian parlour. This postcard of his front sitting room is quite mild in comparison to the bars. In June 1894 Harrison dropped a Victorian bombshell by hanging a sign outside his pub depicting two naked figures. There was a public outcry even though the figures were of Adam and Eve and Harrison was eventually forced to take his sign down in the interests of public modesty.

69. Lincoln has long been noted for its inns. In 1856 there were 75 hostelries with a further 33 beer houses. Another old favourite was the Turks Head Inn, Newport, and in 1877 George Hagues took over as landlord. When he died in 1893, his widow, Mrs. Charlotte Jane Hagues, became the landlady. She was a remarkable woman, not least in that she had twelve children and never ran up more than £20 in Doctors bills throughout her life! Her favourite breakfast was fatty bacon which she liked to choose herself and when she retired in 1906 the old Turks Head was knocked down. This is a photograph of the New Turks Head Hotel which was built on the same site. (Charlotte Hague died in 1936, aged 92!)

70. There has always been a school at Lincoln ever since the cathedral was built. Although the earliest mentions of it place the school below hill. In 1406 the Chapter founded a separate Grammar School for Choristers and in 1906 the whole school moved to its present site on Wragby Road. The name changed and instead of being called The Grammar School, it was known as Lincoln School for the next seventy years. During this time it enjoyed the reputation of a minor public school and admitted boys only. In 1974 it amalgamated with Christ's Hospital School, of Lindum Road, and went comprehensive.

71. Old boys of Lincoln School include Neville Mariner, Basil Boothroyd and John Hurt (the actor). When the new Lincoln School was built in 1906, a preparatory school for the younger boys was also provided. The total cost of the work involved was £20,000 and it was carried out under the able supervision of Leonard Stokes, architect. The preparatory school of which this is a photo comprised of three forms and as it said in a brochure of the time 'the homework set is less than in the senior school'!

72. There was a fives court at Lincoln School although this particular court was very different from
the one which I played on. For a start there are protruberences on the wall and a step in the forecourt;
how on earth this stopped the ball from flying upwards heaven only knows. Also where is the back
wall? This must have been a fag for those boys playing in this particular court constantly having to run
and fetch the ball every five minutes. For the uninitiated fives is a ball game played by hitting the ball
against the wall with gloved hands. But apparently this was an Eton fives court complete with
pepper-box (left-hand side of the court) where the server started the game from.

THE PRISON, LINCOLN.

73. There is no significance in the fact that this postcard follows on from the last three. Lincoln Prison on Greetwell Road was built in 1872 by F. Peck, architect, and was described as 'Castellated Gothic with Romanesque touches'. It replaced the old Castle Prison which in mid-Victorian times was overcrowded beyond belief and prisoners suffered under appalling conditions. The most famous inmate of this particular prison was Eamonn De Valera of Sinn Fein who in the early days of the IRA escaped from Lincoln on 3rd February 1919.

The Cattle Market, Lincoln

74. Lincoln never had a large cattle market in comparison with its neighbouring wold towns although from this postcard (circa 1910) it would seem that the cattle market was still quite busy. Situated on Monk's Road, it used to occupy the site where the College of Technology is today.

Lincoln from the Arboretum.

75. The arboretum was formerly a common land belonging to the freemen of the city and known as Monk's Leys. But the council struck up an agreement whereby the senior freemen would receive £200 per annum on condition that they relinquished their rights to it. As such the arboretum was opened to the public in 1872 by Bishop Wordsworth and Mr. Harrison, the then Mayor.

The Lion
Lincoln Arboretum

76. This strange lion, slightly reminiscent of the Landseer lions underneath Nelson's Column, is one of the noteable features of the arboretum. Made of Coade stone (a kind of terra cotta), it was presented to the city in 1872 by Francis Johnathan Clarke, a Lincoln chemist who was Mayor of Lincoln three times (in 1879, 1884 and 1885). This hapless lion has long been the victim of practical jokes; it was painted in 1909 and again in 1929 by person or persons unknown and more recently has acquired red genitalia.

The Lake, Arboretum, Lincoln

77. A tranquil picture of the arboretum (circa 1912) shows some youngsters feeding the swans around the pond. Those halcyon days of military bands playing in the band stand and women dressed up to the nines in billowing dresses is all part of another age. In 1911 the Mayor, Mr. C. Newsum, officially opened the water supply and to enthusiastic cheers the water shot seventy feet in the air! It is a sad reflection on this day and age to see the state of the pond these days.

The County Hospital, Lincoln.

78. The County Hospital from the south-east shows what a vast hospital this was. Built in 1878 from designs in the Hatfield House style by Alexander Graham, it was enlarged twice. (A popular wing being the Ruston Childrens Ward.) The County replaced an earlier hospital situated in Drury Lane, which is now the local theological college known as the Bishop's Hostel.

79. This cabinet portrait of Lincoln's Christ's Hospital Girls High School Kindergarten was taken by Mr. R. Slingsby, photographer of 168, High Street. Slingsby was a prolific and much admired photographer, who specialised in Victorian portraits. He created an invaluable record of the noteable families, and dignitaries in the city from 1870 to 1900. This particular photograph was taken in 1870.

R. SLINGSBY   LINCOLN

80. William Cottingham was the Mayor of Lincoln in 1877/78 and to mark the event Slingsby recorded Cottingham in his Mayoral paraphernalia. By this time Slingsby had been patronised by his Royal Highness the Prince of Wales Edward VII (as he was quick to point out on the reverse side of his photographic portraits). But the most interesting part about this postcard is that Cottingham is wearing the old Mayoral Chain of Office.

81. Yet another Slingsby study taken much later, in 1893, of
Mr. Shepherd when he was Sheriff of Lincoln. By this time
Slingsby had been awarded four international medals and six
other medals and was much in demand.

82. There has always been a healthy Wesleyan community in Lincoln and one staunch member in Victorian times was James Hall. When he married Elizabeth Goy, the youngest daughter of Matthew Goy (a builder of Grantham Street, Lincoln), G. Hardy of 1, Norman Place, Lincoln took the wedding photographs. He placed the couple against a typical Victorian backcloth (à la Gainsborough) and captured the sort of dress and attire that was the fashion of the day. Incidentally James Hall's father was the captain of one of the steam packets which plied daily between Lincoln and Boston.

83. James Hall married Elizabeth Goy in the Wesleyan Chapel in Clasketgate on the 9th June 1870. Unfortunately this fine building (built in 1836) was demolished in 1963 to make way for a set of offices reminiscent of Alcatraz.

84. At the end of Clasketgate, where it forms the junction with Silver Street, stood the Bulls Head Inn. When the contents of this pub were being sold in 1810, the advertisement which appeared in the press said *To be sold very cheap. A brewing copper, good as new, which will hold four hogsheads; a large cooler; a mash tub, fathering tub, working tub, liquor pump and Troughs, also two hogshead copper and various other brewing utensils. – Apply Mr. Beare, at the Bulls Head Tavern, Lincoln.* This gives a picture of the sort of hardware which every typical eighteenth century pub needed to procure to carry out their business. Noticeably prominent in the foreground is the traffic policeman (complete with white gloves), who had obviously been persuaded off his traffic perch which used to stand in the centre of this busy crossroads where five roads meet.

85. At number 40, Silver Street was the firm of Curtis and Mawer, a well-established firm selling furniture and household items. In 1921 there was a fire which gutted the premises and Mawer Bros (no relation) of Louth were asked to rebuild the shop. In 1922 this was the result, a conglomeration of Edwardian styled art nouveau ideas. It left the building with large panes of glass and ornate carvings, traces of which can still be seen today. Now known as Courts' Furnishers the fascinating feature on the parapet with its rows of little Lincoln Imps together with Brittania have since been removed.

86. Inside Curtis and Mawer there was an impressive staircase complete with aspidistras leading up to the first floor. Sadly this stairway has gone, but the items of furniture left lying about give a good idea of what was in vogue during the twenties. Curtis and Mawer specialised in furniture, carpets, rugs, linoleums, curtains and window fittings and they had two large warehouses at the back of the shop where much of the furniture was made. Even today there is a strange cumbersome looking machine which must weigh some two or three tons which put the stuffing into mattresses.

87. Newport Arch is the only Roman Gateway left in England which is still in use. Originally it had a postern on each side of it, but only one remains; the road which runs underneath Newport Arch is Ermine Street which continues up to the Humber. The house just to the right of the picture is presently owned by Mrs. Downs, who purchased it from a Mr. Lowe (who was head gardener for Shuttleworths). Mr. Shuttleworth gave him this spartan house with damp running riot inside the house and only one cold water tap. It has been tastefully modernised by the Downs yet from the outside looks almost the same today as in this postcard.

88. However, even a Roman Arch could not escape the pitfalls of the twentieth century when in 1964 a lorry practically demolished it. (Mr. Beeching you have much to answer for!) The press of the day tried to be flippant about this tragic episode by conjuring up the cliché 'You cannot put a square peg in a round hole'. Fortunately the damage was repaired.

NEWPORT, ARCH & CATHEDRAL, LINCOLN.

89. In this postcard of Newport Arch from the other side we see just how much the area around it has changed. The Victorian terraces on the left-hand side have been demolished as indeed have the two houses on the right to make way for the Co-operative Society stores, built in 1938. Now serving part of the one way traffic system, this once quiet residential part of Lincoln is now engulfed by commerce and trade.

90. Looking down Bailgate towards Newport Arch there was a fascinating pub known as the George Inn (at 67 Bailgate). Not to be confused with another George Inn on the west side of Bailgate and next door to St. Paul's Churchyard, this inn was leased by the Dean and Chapter. In 1787 it was leased to Isaac Wood, who was gaoler at the castle and by the turn of the century the name had changed to the Three Tuns. (A few Lincolnians of the older generation may remember it.) The Three Tuns had the reputation of being the smallest public house in Lincoln. Incidentally the house on the east side of Newport Arch (the Co-op premises) was also a pub for a short time, known as the Windmill Inn.

91. In the oppsosite direction down Bailgate we see the Lion and Snake public house with the cathedral in the background. Originally these were two separate tenements, the one formerly called 'The Ram' and the other 'The Red Lion' or 'The Lyon in the Bail'. By 1741 these two inns had amalgamated and the snake (an adder) had been added. This curious name is thought to be derived from Psalm 91 v.13. Also the garage, belonging to Mr. Lyon (just a curious coincidence), has been cleared to leave space for the pub car park.

92. Today Bailgate is still as popular a shopping centre as ever it was. This photograph, taken nearly eighty years ago, shows that even then there was an assortment of high class shops. These days the Bailgate area has much to offer the visitor selling such varied items as perfumes, gifts and every brand of whisky known to man.

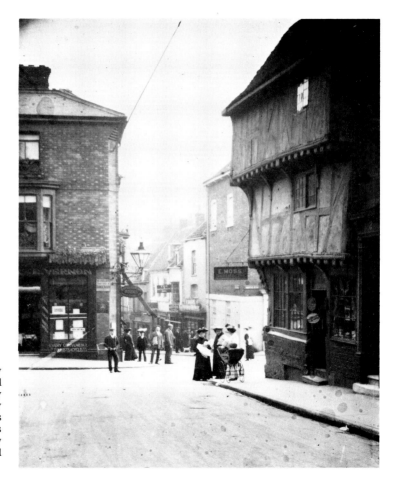

93. At the end of Bailgate, where it is joined by Castle Square, the scene has hardly changed at all in the last hundred years. The building directly opposite was a café and refreshment room run by the Vernon family, catering chiefly for tourers and cyclists. These days the building also caters for tourists although under another guise for now it is a restaurant known as Harvey's Cathedral Restaurant.

94. Once again it is quite remarkable how little this scene has altered. The signs may have changed as different tradesfolk flock to this fahsionable part of Lincoln, but the houses and shops on either side of Steep Hill are still much the same. To the right of this postcard was the frontage of R. Marris (Artistic House and Sign Painter). He was responsible for selling numerous postcards of Lincoln and even had a flourishing trade in images of the Lincoln Imp.

Oct. 14th/04

95. The Old Harlequin Inn was certainly the oldest hostelry in Lincoln and probably one of the oldest in England. The building itself dates from the fourteenth century and was closed ignominiously in 1931, when the building was considered structurally unsafe. Fred Reynolds was the last landlord and when the building was being renovated, he found a two pound cannon ball and a petrified rat complete with tail in one of the chimneys. The building is portrayed in this particularly fine painting, artist unknown, which made a deligthful postcard as opposed to the many photographic views. After its demise as a pub, it became an antiques shop, run by G.W. Shlton, and today is a second hand book shop.

96. Jews House was yet another property owned by the Dean and Chapter. It was named after a Jewess called Belaset De Wallingford, who lived there and was hanged in 1290 for clipping the King's coin. On her death property was given to Walter of Thornton and was used as a family residence for many years. In the last century Mr. Pickering, general broker, occupied the shop to the left of the arched doorway which is currently an intimate and comfortable eating house known as White's Restaurant.

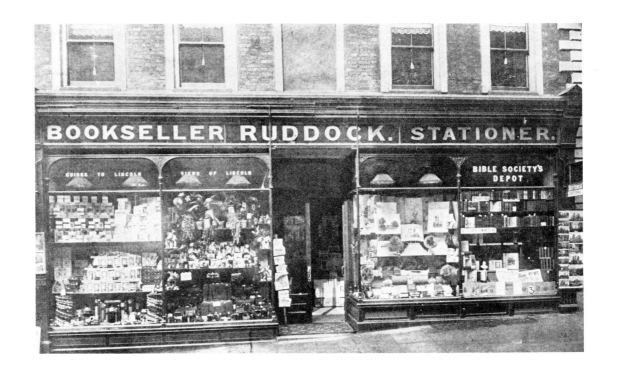

97. In White's Directory of 1856 the firm of Charles Akrill, 159, High Street, was advertised as a bookseller, printer and binder. By the turn of the century the firm had become Ruddocks and Akrill, operating from the same address whilst these days it is simply known as Ruddock's Bookshop. Mr. Jack Ruddock has continued with the tradition of bookselling and this flourishing family business has been responsible for producing many of the cards used in this book.

HIGH STREET & BUTTER MARKET, LINCOLN.

98. At the top of High Street, which leads up to the Strait, there have been several changes. The old Butter Market (to the right of this postcard) was demolished in 1933 along with St. Peter-at-Arches (the church next door) and the Old Blue Boar Inn. To the left of this postcard is Beaumont's Grocers followed by Harston's Music Stores and Bainbridge's Drapery. The equivalent view these days is hardly recognisable.

99. Yet another view of High Street with a close-up of the Butter Market on the right. This fine old building used to house the city assembly rooms on the first floor. Boots the Chemist is prominent halfway down High Street (on the right) at the junction with Clasketgate. Incidentally part of the Butter Market façade was incorporated into the Central Market on Waterside South when it was demolished.

Cornhill, Lincoln.

100. Cornhill with the Corn Exchange in the background (just off High Street) was once a thriving market reminiscent of a busy country market town. The Corn Exchange was opened in 1880 from designs by Bellamy and Hardy (a well-known Lincoln firm of architects). Beneath the Exchange, which had fine accoustic properties, there was a handsome fruit and vegetable market. This scene (circa 1905) is now part of the pedestrian precinct.

101. In 1730 John D'Isney bought some land in Eastgate, just beyond the Close and cleared away part of an old inn (The White Bull) employing Abraham Hayward (a Lincoln builder) to build him a house. At the time that his photograph was taken the house belonged to Mr. Melville J.P., who was the great-great-grandson of John D'Isney. Today the house is a most charming and welcoming hotel run by a Mrs. Payne, who purchased the premises in 1979. Many people have walked straight past the D'Isney because it backs on to the road, but this is the view of the front of the house.

102. Boultham Hall was the home of the Ellison family for many years. The house was built in 1874 and the last private occupant was Colonel Sir Richard Ellison, who died in 1909. Then the Hall was used as a convalescent home for wounded soldiers during the First World War before the city council bought the property in 1929. It was hoped that it might be turned into an old peoples home, but nothing came of this scheme and after lying derelict for some years, the building was demolished. The grounds are now used as one of the city's public parks.

103. For many years Eastcliffe House was the home of one of Lincoln's Victorian captains of industry, Nathaniel Clayton, who with Joseph Shuttleworth established the world renowned engineering firm of Clayton and Shuttleworth. The house was known locally as 'Natty Clayton's Mansion' and it stood in extensive grounds between Lindum Road and Eastcliffe Road. It was built in 1877 at a cost of between £40,000 and £50,000 and was demolished in 1926.

104. At the junction of Doddington Road and Newark Road is a fine example of Victorian architecture known as 'Redlands' House. Presently the home of Mr. & Mrs. Stockmarr, this Victorian family residence (built in 1866) was modelled on 'Lindum House', Wellington Road, Nantwich, Cheshire. For some years it was the home of Eric Stapleton (the estate agent), who restored much of it. Even so it is odd to think that there are two houses on either side of the Pennines which are both exactly the same.

105. In 1728 Sir John Monson was created Baron Monson of Burton. To mark the event he demolished the existing Tudor House which once stood on this site and erected a massive Hall, seen here. The south front (to the left of the picture) was added in 1767 and sadly this is the only remaining vestige of a once impressive country seat.

106. It would appear from this small book that there were a lot large houses in and around Lincoln and indeed there were. This one of Monks Manor (just off Greetwell Road) was built for Joseph Ruston in 1870 and is typical. Its design smacks of Osbourne (Queen Victoria's country cottage on the Isle of Wight). Charles Pratt, the wine merchant, bought Monks Manor in 1912 and lived there until his death in 1932 when it was pulled down.

107. The original church of St. Swithin's was built only a few yards away from where its successor stands today. The first church to St. Swithin was destroyed by fire in 1644 when some soldiers in the Civil War were drying some gunpowder near the Church and inadvertently let it explode. Then for the next 250 years the site was used as a sheep market until the present church was built from designs by Mr. James Fowler of Louth.

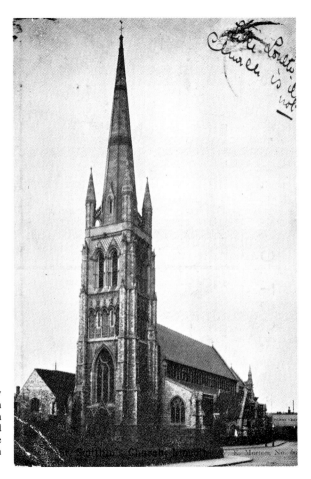

108. The mediaeval church of St. Benedict, which was not used in the 1900's, has still been left standing. The ivy has long been cleared away and Lincoln's War Memorial now stands in front of it. How this church has escaped being moved, demolished or 'modernised' is a complete mystery.

St. Benedict's Church, Lincoln.

109. Another glimpse of St. Benedicts Church practically covered over in creeper. The row of cabs and carts to the side of this church indicated that parking was something of a problem, even in Edwardian times. The pinnacle in the distance belonged to the Thomas Cooper Memorial Baptist Chapel, erected in 1885, and the offices to the left are those of the Lincolnshire Echo.

110. Lincoln Public Library in Free School Lane was opened on the 24th February 1914. Largely paid for by a gift of £10,000 from Andrew Carnegie, the Scottish/American millionaire, it replaced Lincoln's first public library which had been accommodated in the old City Assembly Rooms above the Butter Market in the High Street. The new library was designed by Sir Reginald Blomfield, who also designed the water tower in Westgate and the Usher Art Gallery. The library was opened by a distinguished old boy of Lincoln Grammar School, Dr. T.E. Page (of the Loeb Classical Library).

111. There was a time when pavement artists were the norm rather than the exception; the equivalent these days might be the numerous buskers and music merchants which plague the London Underground. This nameless Leonardo had a patch the corner of St. Mary-le-Wigford and from the standard of his work it would appear that he could put many modern artists to shame.

ST. MARY-LE-WIGFORD CHURCH, LINCOLN.

Copyright.

112. St. Mary-le-Wigford was built in the ancient district of Wigford or Wickford – hence the name. There are two brasses in the church, one to William Horn, Mayor of Lincoln 1469, and the other to John Jobson, an alderman who died in 1525. St. Mary's Conduit in the foreground has a sign on it which says 'set up by the inhabitants of the South Ward of the City and supplied with water in 1540'. Believed to have been built from fragments of the Whitefriars, which formerly stood on the site of St. Mark's Station.

113. This postcard of Timothy Wilson, Boot and Shoe dealer, was taken circa 1910. Adam Spencer was the manager although it is more probable that the gent in this photograph was Timothy Wilson himself. The shop was next door to 'The Treaty of Commerce' pub in High Street.

South Bar, Lincoln

114. Looking down South Park Avenue from South Bar we see the Common to the right of this postcard and just what problems the traffic caused. This scene is practically unrecognisable today as the increased traffic flow rushes through the roundabout now on this junction. Particularly sad is the disappearance of the very ornate gas lamp, which used to stand in the middle of the road.

South Park, Lincoln.

115. On this pictorial jaunt around Lincoln the continuation down South Park Avenue looked like this with playing fields on the right and a pretty row of trees bordering the road of this once quiet suburb.

116. At the end of South Park Avenue is the Canwick Hill roundabout and just a short way up the hill is where this photograph was taken. Showing numerous industrial chimneys which cut up the panorama like a knife, it demonstrates Lincoln's heavy emphasis on industry. Just visible in the middle distance is the firm of Robey and Co.

117. 'I'll send you to Bracebridge!' might have been the retort of an exasperated parent. It was the penultimate threat, but it seemed to work. For this was the lunatic asylum and nothing could be worse from the look of this postcard; this was only the medical Superintendant's house and that looks gruesome enough.

118. In complete contrast this pretty picture of the boats at Bracebridge, taken before the First World War, illustrates a leisurely way of life. The River Witham had several points where skiffs and rowing boats could be hired; this particular spot was just outside the Plough Inn (the steps on the left-hand side led up to it).

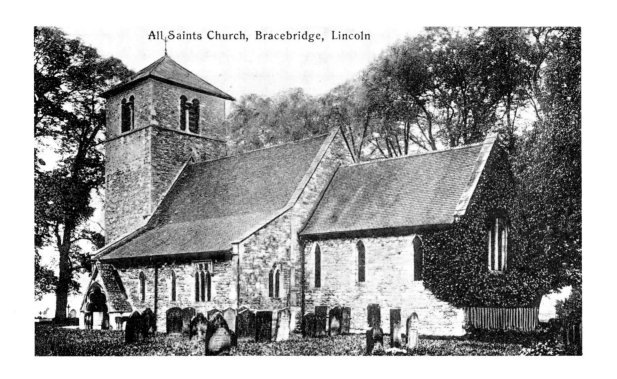

All Saints Church, Bracebridge, Lincoln

119. The mediaeval Church of All Saints, Bracebridge was incorporated into the city just over sixty years ago. The tower of the church is either late Saxon or early Norman and in the wall at the west end of the south aisle is a 'Leper squint' (a narrow window through which lepers, standing outside, could watch the service).

120. On the 27th June 1958 her Majesty Queen Elizabeth II and Prince Philip visited Lincoln cathedral. They are pictured here leaving by the judgement porch in the company of Bishop Dunlop (Dean of Lincoln) and Bishop Riches (Bishop of Lincoln). Judgement porch is the popular name for the south portal of this beautiful retrochoir. The reason for this Royal visit was the official opening of Pelham Bridge.

121. No book on Lincoln would be complete without mentioning the Lincoln Imp. The city has a fiercely independant community and the Imp is to Lincoln what Robin Hood was to Nottingham. This ugly little mascot has appeared on countless badges, toasting forks, shoe horns and postcards. There was a public outcry recently when Lincoln County Council wanted to 'dump the Imp'; like Lincoln Green Cloth this symbol has become famous throughout the world. Higgs Bros., the tobacconist of the Stonebow (they also had shops in Spilsby, Sleaford and Louth), said that 'the Imp was the slogan of Lincoln' and added 'If you must smoke a pipe — see that it's an Imp!'

122. Out of all the questions which visitors ask when they look round this vast cathedral probably the most popular is 'Where's the toilet?' or 'Do you serve coffee?'. But inevitably they ask 'Where's the Lincoln Imp?'. Well it's here! On the top of the pillar on the right of this postcard. The Angel Choir itself is one of the most exquisite pieces of architecture ever built.

123. Rememberance Day in Lincoln cathedral when we reflect how hard our armed forces fought to give us the freedom we now enjoy and how hard those insidious forces within our society today try to take it away.

Lincoln at Sunset.

124. Lincoln's crowning glory is without doubt its cathedral! With the River Witham meandering peacefully by in the foreground, it makes a perfect picture. It must have been a scene like this that prompted John Ruskin (1819-1900) to comment: *I have always held and am prepared against all comers to maintain that the cathedral of Lincoln is out and out the most precious piece of architecture in the British Isles and roughly speaking worth any two other cathedrals we have.*